od • A beautiful day f... or.
mine? • It's a neighborly day in this
beauty. • Would you be mine? • Could
o have a neighbor just like you! • I've
od with you, • So . . . • Let's make the
e're together, we might as well say
mine? • Won't you be my neighbor?
• Please won't you be my neighbor?
od • A beautiful day for a neighbor.
mine? • It's a neighborly day in this
beauty. • Would you be mine? • Could
o have a neighbor just like you! • I've
od with you, • So . . . • Let's make the
e're together, we might as well say
mine? • Won't you be my neighbor?
• Please won't you be my neighbor?

A
Beautiful Day
in the
Neighborhood

A Beautiful Day in the Neighborhood

The Poetry of Mister Rogers

Lyrics by
FRED ROGERS

Illustrations by
LUKE FLOWERS

QUIRK BOOKS
PHILADELPHIA

Contents

My name is Mister Rogers.

I'm glad that you are near.

You've made this day a special day

By just your being here.

—From the opening song of the Canadian show *Misterogers*,
the precursor of *Mister Rogers' Neighborhood*

Welcome to the Neighborhood

Won't You Be My Neighbor?

It's a beautiful day in this neighborhood
A beautiful day for a neighbor.
Would you be mine?
Could you be mine?

It's a neighborly day in this beauty wood
A neighborly day for a beauty.
Would you be mine?
Could you be mine?

I have always wanted to have a neighbor just like you!
I've always wanted to live in a neighborhood with you,
    So . . .

Let's make the most of this beautiful day
Since we're together, we might as well say
Would you be mine?
Could you be mine?

Won't you be my neighbor?
Won't you please,
Won't you please?
Please won't you be my neighbor?

Mister Rogers' Invitation

Would you like to meet the tiger
Who lives there in that clock?
Or see that Eiffel Tower
And hear a French man talk?

Would you like to use a telephone?
It's a tin can on a string
That lets you reach the castle
Where a most majestic king
His Majesty King Friday
  is in charge of everything!

Would you like to ride a trolley
Along that trolley track?
Or crawl right through the underpass—
Right through and then right back?

Then pop into this house here,
Come in and visit me.
There's lots for us to see and hear
And think and do and feel and be.

My name is Mister Rogers.
I'm glad that you are near.
You've made this day a special day
By just your being here.

Be the Best of Whatever You Are

If you can't be a pine
On the top of a hill
Be a shrub in the valley, but be
The best little shrub by the side of the rill.

If you can't be a woods
Be a tree.
If you can't be a highway
Then just be a trail.
If you can't be the sun
Be a star.

It isn't by size that you win or you fail.
Be the best of whatever you are.
Be the best of whatever you are!

I Like You as You Are

I like you as you are
Exactly and precisely!
I think you turned out nicely
And I like you as you are.

I like you as you are
Without a doubt or question
Or even a suggestion
'Cause I like you as you are.

I like your disposition
Your facial composition
And with your kind permission
I'll shout it to a star.

I like you as you are
I wouldn't want to change you
Or even rearrange you
Not by far.

I like you, I-L-I-K-E-Y-O-U.
I like you, yes I do,
I like you, Y-O-U.
I like you, like you as you are.

Lyrics by Josie Carey, Music by Fred Rogers

I Think I'm Going to Like Today

I think I'm going to like today
I think I'll call it fine
I'll wrap it in ribbons
And make it mine.

I think I'm going to like today
It's very plain to see
I like every minute
And it likes me.

Don't you agree?
This is the nicest day in the neighborhood
The nicest day in the calendar
The nicest day in the hemisphere for me.

I think I'm going to like today
It's been the best by far.
I got it by wishing
On last night's star.

I think I'm going to like today
And when today is through
I'll catch it and keep it
As good as new.

I'll have the nicest day in the neighborhood
The nicest day in the calendar
The nicest day will just stay at home with me.
I think I'm going to like today.

I Give a Hoot for You

Oh, I give a hoot for you
'Cause golly, you're neat!
Yes, I give a hoot for you
You simply couldn't be beat.

        You're nice as pie and really, I
        Don't know when, why, or what!
        But I've got to say, that in every way,
        You're my "fa-vo-rut."

Oh, I give a hoot for you
You're swell, that's how I feel!
Yes, I give a hoot for you
You're absolutely for real.

I'm hoping, too, as I hoot for you
That you will soon agree
To hoot and howl like this wise old owl
And give a hoot for me: "Hoot!"

Lyrics by Josie Carey, Music by Fred Rogers

Children Can

Who can crawl under a table?
Who can sit under a chair?
Who can fit their feet in little shoes
And sleep most anywhere?
Who can play very much longer
Play much harder than grownups ever dare?
You're a child so you can do it.
You can do it anywhere!

Who can wake up every morning
And be ready right away?
Who can notice all the tiny things
That other people say?
Who can make the things they play with
Something different for every single day?
You're a child and you can do it.
You can do it any way!

Roll in the grass
Squoosh in the mud
Lick an ice cream cone
Sing to a bass
Splash in a flood
By a stepping stone . . .
    all alone.

Who can put your hand in my hand
And be ready to feel all safe and strong?
You're a child so you can do it.
Children do it all life long!

It's Good to Talk

It's good to talk
It's good to say the things we feel
It's good to talk.
We're much more real without the lot.

It's good to talk
It's good to find someone to trust
It's good to talk.
We know we must do more than balk.

People weren't born to be silent
Our tongues make wonderful sounds.
Just try a few phrases for practice
You'll see there are very few bounds.

Let's see now: "I like you. I'm angry.
I'm happy. I'm sad."
You see? That's not bad.
It's good, not bad.

It's good to talk.
It's good to say the things we mean.
It's good to talk of all we've seen and heard and felt for
And wished and knelt for.

We need to talk more.
It's good to talk.

Things Are Different

You never know the story
By the cover of the book.
You can't tell what a dinner's like
By simply looking at the cook.
It's something everybody needs to know
Way down deep inside
That things are often different
Than the way they look.

When I put on a costume
To play a fancy part
That costume changes just my looks.
It doesn't change my heart.
You cannot know what someone's thinking
By the picture you just took
'Cause things are often different
From the way they look.

A Place of My Own

I like to have a place of my own
A place where I can be by myself.
When I want to think and play by myself
I like to have a place of my own.

I like to have a place of my own
A step on a staircase, a drawer or a chair,
A corner, a spot anywhere,
A place I can call my own.

Dishes have places
So do pots and pans
Beds and bathtubs
Shoes and socks.

Tables have places
So do faces and hands.
Houses have places
Keys have locks.

I like to have a place of my own
A place where I can be by myself.
When I want to play and think by myself
I like to have a place of my own.

Smile in Your Pocket

There's a smile in your pocket
There's a smile up your sleeve
There's a smile in your pocket
And it isn't make-believe.

There's a smile in your pocket
There's a smile in your shoe
There's a smile in your pocket
Without anything to do.

Now, a pocket is handy for candy
    And dandy for string.
A pocket is nifty for folks who are thrifty
With wrappers and rings—
All sorts of things.

But a smile in your pocket
Feels a bit out of place
'Cause a smile in your pocket
Wants to be on your face!

Lyrics by Josie Carey, Music by Fred Rogers

You Are You

I eat and you do, too.
You sleep and I do, too.
I wake up and you do, too.
So we two do so much the same—
But I'm Mister Rogers
And you have your name.

You are you and I am I
And we will always be
Quite different to people who know us well
'Cause they're the ones who like us to be different.

You are you and I am I
And we will never be
Exactly like anybody else
'Cause everybody else is different.
Different, different, we are different.
Isn't it great?
To be different!

You and I and he and she
    And isn't it great to be you and I?
And we will always be
Quite different to people who know us well.
'Cause they're the ones who like us
They really want us
They're the ones who like us to be different.

What Do You Do with the Mad That You Feel?

What do you do with the mad that you feel
When you feel so mad you could bite?
When the whole wide world seems oh so wrong
And nothing you do seems very right?

What do you do? Do you punch a bag?
Do you pound some clay or some dough?
Do you round up friends for a game of tag?
Or see how fast you go?

It's great to be able to stop
When you've planned a thing that's wrong
And be able to do something else instead
And think this song:

I can stop when I want to
Can stop when I wish
I can stop, stop, stop anytime.
And what a good feeling to feel like this
And know that the feeling is really mine.

Know that there's something deep inside
That helps us become what we can.
For a girl can be someday a woman
And a boy can be someday a man.

I Love to Shine

I love to shine, I love to shine
I love to let what's in me
    Shine outside.
I love to shine, I love to shine
I love to let what's in me
    Shine outside.

The world needs all the light
    That we can muster
Each moon and star and comet
    In the sky.

We add to all the world
    Our special luster
So shine on, friends,
    And never question why.

We love to shine,
    We love to shine.
We love to let what's in us
    Shine outside.
We love to let what's in us
    Shine outside.

33

Fences

Fences, fences, the world is full of fences
And some I like
And some I don't like
That keep me out.
Now the kind that keep me out
Are the kind that make me pout.
They're the kind that have no gate at all.
They're the kind that go up too tall.

Fences, fences, the world is full of fences
And some I like.
Yes, some I do like.
The kind that keep me safe.
Now, the kind that keep me safe, you see
Are the kind that keep wild beasts from me.
They're the kind that help me stop my car
So I never have to go too far.

Fences, fences, the world is full of fences.
From what I see
They're a help to me.
And the ones I hate
I can tolerate.
So, fences, fences
The world must keep its

many
many
fences.

Doing Song

Clap your hands
Blow a kiss
Make a face
Like this!

Snap your thumbs
Shake your head
Make-believe
You're in bed.

Blink your eyes
Stretch your arms
Stand up straight
Look for farms.

Here's the horse (*Neigh!*)
Here's the cow (*Moooo!*)
Here's the sheep (*Baaaa!*)
You can bow.

Here's the duck (*Quack quack!*)
Here's the cat (*Meow!*)
Here's the dog (*Bark!*)
Here's your hat.

Wave goodbye
Drive the car
Throw the ball
Throw it far.

Eat your meal
Sing a song
Brush your teeth
Hear ding-dong!

Hug your pillow
Click the light
Hug yourself
Say goodnight. (*Goodnight!*)

Les Jours de la Semaine
(The Days of the Week)

In France the days are just the same,
   The same as over here.
The sun goes up and then comes down
Each week and month and year.

But since the French speak differently
Their days don't sound the same.
What say we learn it their way?
I think that would be tame.

The first day is *Lundi*
Monday's what we say.
The next day is *Mardi*
In English that's Tuesday.

Wednesday is *Mercredi*.
      Then *Jeudi* comes your way.
What's the French for Friday?
Vendredi, they say.

The weekend starts with *Samedi*.
That's Saturday, you know.
Dimanche is French for Sunday.
      Where did that whole week go?

Lundi, Mardi, Mercredi, Jeudi,
      Vendredi, Samedi, Dimanche.
That's fun, don't you agree?

Lyrics by Josie Carey, Music by Fred Rogers

39

Take My Time

I like to take my time.
I mean that when I want to do a thing
I like to take my time to do it right.
I mean I might just make mistakes
If I should have to hurry up.

And so I like to take my time
To tie my shoes, to eat, to get dressed
To go to sleep at night, to sing a song for you
And everything I like to do.

I like to take my time.
I mean that when I want to do a thing
I like to take my time to do it well.
I mean I might just make mistakes
If I should have to hurry up and so
I like to take my time.

What Can You Hear?

What can you hear
    When you close your eyes
When you close your eyes
    And listen a while.
Can you hear? Can you hear?

Can you hear the love, the anger, the joy
The sadness, the fear?
Can you hear the whisper of someone
    Who wants to be very near?

What can you hear
    When you close your eyes?

Can you hear

    a birdie

    singing a song

in the skies?

    Can you hear?

I'm Busy Being Busy

I'm busy being busy
Yes, the calendar's my task.
I'm busy giving dates away
To all who come and ask
For a week for this, a week for that.

I'm busy being busy
And the busier I get
The more some people need a week
For barbershop quartets, and a week
For tuna fish croquettes.

I found a week for cheddar cheese
For fleas and Spanish onions.
I found a week for willow trees
And bees and curing bunions.
I searched with purple passion
For a national event
Calling the world's attention
To the day the pretzel first was bent.

And I gave a special Groundhog's Day
To please dear Punxsutawney.
I gave a week to Turtle Creek,
A day to sing of Swanee.
I made a special leap year, too
And a day for wearing navy blue.
Oh, you'll never know how much I do
I'm busy being busy.

I'm busy being busy
And the busier I am
The more some people need a week
For elderberry jam, or a week
For naming babies Sam.

I'm busy being busy
And the busier I seem
The more I'm called upon to give
A day to sour cream, or a week
To pantomime
Or bells that chime
I don't have time
To even end this rhyme.
I'm very busy!

Lyrics by Josie Carey, Music by Fred Rogers

I Did, Too

Did you ever fall and hurt your hand or knee?
Did you ever bite your tongue?
Did you ever find the stinger of a bee
Stuck in your thumb?
I did, too.

It seems the things that you do
I did, too
When I was very new.
I had lots of hurts and scares and worries
When I was growing up like you.

Did you ever trip and fall down on the stairs?
Did you ever stub your toe?
Did you ever dream of great big grizzly bears
Who wouldn't go?
I did, too.

It seems the things that you do
I did, too
When I was very new.
I had lots of hurts and scares and worries
When I was growing up like you.

Sometimes Isn't Always

Sometimes I DON'T feel like combing my hair.
I DON'T feel like washing my face sometimes.
Sometimes I DON'T feel like saying "okay."
But sometimes isn't always.

Sometimes I DO feel like combing my hair.
I DO feel like washing my face sometimes.
Sometimes I DO feel like saying "okay."
But sometimes isn't always.

Sometimes I DON'T feel like going to bed.
I DO feel like getting right up sometimes.
Sometimes I DON'T feel like wearing my shoes.
But sometimes isn't always.

Sometimes I DON'T feel like sometimes I DO.
I feel like I DON'T like to feel sometimes.
Sometimes I DON'T . . . and sometimes I DO.
But sometimes isn't always
Isn't always
Isn't always.

Everybody's Shy Sometimes

Did you ever feel so shy
You thought you'd hide
You thought you'd hide
Beside your mom
Beside your dad?

Did you ever feel so shy
You wondered why
You wondered why
You didn't cry
You just felt shy?

Everyone feels a little shy sometimes
Even if you're big and tall.
Everyone thinks a little shy sometimes.
Everyone feels a little small sometimes.
Everyone feels a little shy.

I'd Like to Be Like Mom and Dad

I'd like to be just like my mom
She's loving and she's bright.
She knows just how to care for me
And works to make things right.

And Daddy likes the things she does
The way she looks, and gee!
I'd like to be just like my mom
And have someone like me.

I'd like to be just like my dad
He's wise and he is kind.
He knows just how to help me grow
And does his work just fine.

And Mommy likes the things he does
The way he looks, and gee!
I'd like to be just like my dad
And have someone like me.

You Can Never Go
Down the Drain

You can never go down
Can never go down
Can never go down the drain.

You're bigger than the water.
You're bigger than the soap.
    You're much bigger than all the

bubbles.

So you see . . .

You can never go down

Can never go down

the drain!

Can never go down

The Clown in Me

A clown, a clown
I think I'll be a clown.
I think I'll make the people laugh
And laugh all over town.
A clown, that's what I'll be. A clown!

Sometimes I feel when I'm afraid
That I will never make the grade.
So I pretend I'm someone else
And show the world my other self.
I'm not quite sure of me, you see
When I have to make a clown of me.

A clown, a clown
I think I'll be a clown.
I think I'll make the people laugh
And laugh all over town.
A clown, that's what I'll be. A clown!

Sometimes I feel all good inside
And haven't got a thing to hide.
My friends all tell me I'm the best
They think I'm better than the rest.
It's times like this I act myself
And I let the clown stay on the shelf.

Myself, myself
I think I'll be myself.
I think I'll let the people see
The comfortable inside of me.
Myself . . . I'll be myself!

It's only when I feel let down
I might be scared into a clown.
But he can be himself
When I can be . . .
Myself, myself
I think I'll be myself!

We Are Elephants

You can tell at once
We are elephants.
We are elephants big and strong.
From the backs and fronts
We are elephants.
We're elephants all day long.

From the tip of the tusk to the knee
We are elephantinus as can be.
From the trunks to our tails you can see
We're a ponderous, prosperous,
    pompous, preposterous
Pachyderm family of three.

You can smell at once
We are elephants.
We are elephants, come what may.
And we yell at once:
"We are elephants!
And it's elephants we will stay!"

Summer Rain

The sun is sad and I am glad
My flower has needed the rain.
The summer sky's been awfully dry
My flower just had to complain.

I know it's wet as it can get
But listen and let me explain:
If you were a flower
You'd wish for a shower—
A lovely summer rain.

My flower's bed was hard as lead
Before we had this summer rain.
My flower's head was bowed and red
I think she had cause to complain.

And then the sky began to cry
And water poured down once again.
Although we are wetter
My flower feels better—
She loves the summer rain.

It's an Ugly Day

It's an ugly day
Made of mugly gray
It's a sit-down-by-the-fire
And be snuggly day.

It's a cloudy day
And a dowdy day
It's a play-some-Chinese-checkers
Read-out-loud day.

It's a day to cuddle up
With a chocolate cookie
Hook a rug or knit—
'Cause it's an ugly day
Made of mugly gray
It's a better-wear-your-sweater
And be snuggly day.

If we pop us some corn
And have cinnamon toast
I'd say we'd made the most
Of an ugly day.

I'm Glad I'm the Way I Am

I'm glad I'm the way I am
I'm glad I'm me.
I'm glad I'm the way
That I'm supposed to be.

I like how I look
I like the way that I feel
I feel that I have a right to be
Quite pleased with me.

I'm glad I'm the way I am
I think I'm fine.
I'm glad I'm the way I am
The pleasure's mine.

It's good that I look the way I should
Wouldn't change now if I could
'Cause I'm happy to be me!

Walking Giraffe

I love to take my giraffe
for walks

He's taller
than anyone else
I know.

You're welcome to talk
with my
tall giraffe

He's kind
from his head
to his toe.

So step up
and speak to
my pet giraffe,

He'll talk to us down
here below.

I'm Still Myself Inside

I can put on a hat or put on a coat
Or wear a pair of glasses or sail in a boat.
I can change all my names
And find a place to hide.
I can do almost anything but
I'm still myself inside.

I can go far away or dream anything
Or wear a scary costume or act like a king.
I can change all my names
And find a place to hide.
I can do almost anything but
I'm still myself
I'm still myself
I'm still myself inside.

Everything Grows Together

Everything grows together

Because you're all one piece.

Your toes grow

As your feet grow

As your legs grow

As your fingers grow

As your hands grow

As your arms grow

As your ears grow

As your nose grows

As the rest of you grows

Because you're all one piece!

It Hurts to Be Lonely

It hurts so much to be lonely
And there's no one else around.
There's no one who really cares for me
Nowhere to be found.

Oh, what I'd give for another chance
Now that I know I was wrong.
And wouldn't it be simply wonderful
If someone came along who knows
It hurts so much to be lonely.

Oh how happy I could be
If that special someone held my hand
And said, "Come, be with me."
It hurts so much to be lonely.
Oh, how life can be so cruel
But I only have myself to blame.
Why was I such a fool?

Oh what I'd give for another chance
Now that I know I was wrong.
And wouldn't it be simply wonderful
If someone came along who knows
It hurts so much to be lonely.

Oh, how happy I could be
If that special someone held my hand
And said, "Come, be with me."

Are You Brave?

Are you brave and don't know it?
Are you brave and can't tell?
Are you brave and just don't show it
While others know it very well?

Are you brave and you wonder?
Are you brave and you doubt?
Are you brave above and under
Especially when you're inside out?

Tell me,
Won't you tell me?
Tell me,
Are you brave?

Parents Were Little Once, Too

It's great for me to remember
As I put away my toys
That mothers were all little girls one time
And fathers were all little boys.

My daddy seems so big right now
He must have grown a lot.
Imagine how he felt one day
When he was just a tot.

My mother's not so big as Dad
But bigger than my sister.
I wonder if she ever had
A little fever blister.

It's great for me to remember
As I put away my toys
That mothers were all little girls one time
And fathers were all little boys.

Did You Know?

Did you know? Did you know?
Did you know that it's all right to wonder?
Did you know that it's all right to wonder?
There are all kinds of wonderful things!

Did you know? Did you know?
Did you know that it's all right to marvel?
Did you know that it's all right to marvel?
There are all kinds of marvelous things!

You can ask a lot of questions about the world
And your place in it.
You can ask about people's feelings;
You can learn the sky's the limit.

Did you know? Did you know?
Did you know when you wonder you're learning?
Did you know when you marvel you're learning?
About all kinds of wonderful,
About all kinds of marvelous,
Marvelously wonderful things?

It's You I Like

It's you I like.
It's not the things you wear
It's not the way you do your hair
But it's you I like.

The way you are right now
The way down deep inside you
Not the things that hide you
Not your toys
They're just beside you.

But it's you I like.
Every part of you
Your skin, your eyes, your feelings
Whether old or new.

I hope that you'll remember
Even when you're feeling blue
That it's you I like
It's you yourself
It's you—

It's you I like!

What Do You Think Is Important?

What, what, what do you think
What do you think is important? (Really.)
What, what, what do you think
What do you think really counts?

What do you think about other people?
What do you think about new ideas?
What, what, what do you think
What do you think is important?

Some people think that houses and cars
And lots of fancy toys
Are things that are most important
For grown-up girls and boys.

Of course, houses are nice if there's love inside
And cars are, too, if they run well.
It's the things that we do with the toys that we have
That help us to feel that we've done well.

What, what, what do you think
What do you think is important? (Really.)
What, what, what do you think
What do you think is the best?

What kind of world would you like to live in?
What kind of love would you like to give?
What is essential for you and your neighbor?
What, what, what do you think
What do you think is important?

Many Ways to Say I Love You

There are many ways to say "I love you."
There are many ways to say "I care about you."
Many ways, many ways, many ways to say
"I love you."

There's the cooking way to say "I love you."
There's the cooking something someone really likes to eat.
The cooking way, the cooking way, the cooking way to say
"I love you."

There's the eating way to say "I love you."
There's the eating something someone made especially.
The eating way, the eating way, the eating way to say
"I love you."

Cleaning up a room can say "I love you."
Hanging up a coat before you're asked to.
Drawing special pictures for the holidays and
Making plays.

There are many ways to say "I love you."
Just by being there when things are sad and scary, just by
Being there, being there, being there to say
"I love you."

You'll find many ways to say "I love you."
You'll find many ways to understand what love is.
Many ways, many ways, many ways to say
"I love you."

Cooking, eating
Cleaning, drawing
Playing, being
Understanding
Love you.

Please Don't Think It's Funny

Sometimes you feel like holding your pillow all night long.
Sometimes you hug your teddy bear tightly
He's old but he's still strong.
And sometimes you want to snuggle up closely
With your own mom and dad.
At night, you even need the light sometimes
But that's not bad.

Please don't think it's funny
When you want an extra kiss.
There are lots and lots of people
Who sometimes feel like this.
Please don't think it's funny
When you want the ones you miss.
There are lots and lots of people
Who sometimes feel like this.

It's great to know you're growing up bigger every day.
But somehow things you like to remember
Are often put away.
And sometimes you wonder over and over
If you should stay inside.
When you enjoy a younger toy
You never need to hide.

In the long, long trip of growing
There are stops along the way
For thoughts of all the soft things
And a look at yesterday.

For a chance to fill our feelings
With comfort and with ease
And then tell the new tomorrow
"You can come now when you please."

So please don't think it's funny
When you want an extra kiss.
There are lots and lots of people
Who sometimes feel like this.
Please don't think it's funny
When you want the ones you miss.
There are lots and lots of people
Who sometimes feel like this.

Let's Be Together Today

Let's go right away, go somewhere today
Let's be together and stay and stay.
Let's go together today, right away.
Let's be together today!

Together's the way I like the best.
I like to be with you.
I like the things you explain to me—
The things you show me to do.

Let's go right away, go somewhere today
Let's be together and stay and stay.
Let's go together today.

Right away, let's be together today.

Some days it's good to play alone
But sometimes I get bored.
There's just so much you can do yourself
With a ball or a doll or a sword.

But whenever I hear you've got some time
And want me to be with you,
I wonder how you knew
'Cause that's what I wanted, too!

Let's go right away, go somewhere today

Let's be together and stay and stay.

Let's go together today right away.

Let's be together today!

You're Growing

You used to creep and crawl real well
But then you learned to walk real well.
There was a time you'd coo and cry
But then you learned to talk, and, my!
You hardly ever cry
You hardly ever crawl at all
I like the way you're growing up.
It's fun! That's all!

You're growing, you're growing
You're growing in and out.
You're growing, you're growing
You're growing all about.

Your hands are getting bigger now.
Your arms and legs are longer now.
You even sense your insides grow
When Mom and Dad refuse you, so
You're learning how to wait now.
It's great to hope and wait somehow.
I like the way you're growing up.
It's fun! That's all!

You're growing, you're growing
You're growing in and out.
You're growing, you're growing
You're growing all about.

Your friends are getting bigger now.
They're better every day somehow.
You used to stay at home to play
But now you even play away.
You do important things now.
Your friends and you do big things now.
I like the way you're growing up.
It's fun! That's all!

You're growing, you're growing
You're growing in and out.
You're growing, you're growing
You're growing all about.

Someday you'll be a grown-up, too
And have some children grow up, too.
Then you can love them in and out
And tell them stories all about
The times when you were their size
The times when you found great surprise
In growing up. And they will sing:
"It's fun! That's all."

You're growing, you're growing
You're growing in and out.
You're growing, you're growing
You're growing all about.

Some Things
I Don't Understand

Some things I don't understand.
Some things are scary and sad.
Sometimes I even get bad when I'm mad.
Sometimes I even get glad.

Why does a dog have to bark?
Why does an elephant die?
Why can't we play all the time in the park?
Why can't my pussycat fly?
    Why,
              why,
  why,
              why,
                      why,
                why?
                        I wonder why.

Why do fire engines make noise?
Why is hot water so hot?
Why aren't live babies like my other toys?
Why do I wonder a lot?

Someday, oh someday, I'll know what to say.
Someday, oh someday, I'll not have to say
"Why?"

When a Baby Comes

When a baby comes to your house
It's a girl or it's a boy.
It's a sister or a brother,
But it's never just a toy.

It can cry and it can holler.
It can wet and it can coo.
But there's one thing it can never—
It can never be like you.

You were there before the baby.
Now the baby's always there.
Now you wait for special moments
With your mother in the chair.

You're a very special person.
You are special to your mom.
And your dad begins to say, "You'll
Always be the older one."

It's so good to know that always
There's a special place for you.
And a special place for baby
Right inside the family, too.

You've a place that no one else has.
There is only one like you.

The King and the Ocean

"I have a notion
To move to the ocean!"
Declared a king in his tower
After thinking for an hour.
He traveled for days around his land
But he couldn't find an ocean at hand.
Finally, the king returned to his tower.
He thought and thought for another hour,
Then said he so loud and clear
So all could hear,
"You know, I'm fond of my own pond.
I think I'll stay right here!"

Sometimes I Wonder If I'm a Mistake

Sung by Daniel Striped Tiger

Sometimes I wonder if I'm a mistake
I'm not like anyone else I know.
When I'm asleep or even awake
Sometimes I get to dreaming that
I'm just a fake.

I'm not like anyone else.
Others I know are big and are wild.
I'm very small and quite tame.
Most of the time I'm weak and I'm mild.
Do you suppose that's a shame?

Often I wonder if I'm a mistake.
I'm not supposed to be scared, am I?
Sometimes I cry and sometimes I shake
Wondering "Isn't it true
That the strong never break?"

I'm not like anyone else I know
I'm not like anyone else.

Sung by Lady Aberlin

I think you are just fine as you are.
I really must tell you
I do like the person that you are becoming.
When you are sleeping,
When you are waking,
You are my friend.
It's really true.
I like you.
Crying or shaking or dreaming or breaking
There's no one mistaking it!
You're my best friend.
You're not a fake.
You're no mistake.
You are my friend.

A Bird-Watching Song

I am the merry bird-watcher
I watch them through my telescope.
I watch them as they build their nests
And gather food and sing and rest.
I raise my telescope to my eyes
And watch the birds as they fly by.
And from this angle I can see
The birds as they fly merrily.

You Are Special

You are my friend,
You are special.
You are my friend,
You're special to me.

You are the only one like you.
Like you, my friend, I like you.
In the daytime
In the nighttime
Anytime that you feel's the right time
For a friendship with me, you see

F - R - I - E - N - D

special.

You are my friend,
You're special to me.
There's only one
In this wonderful world.

You
are
special.

Creation Duet

What made the rainbow and the sky?
What made the bird and let it fly?
What made the hour, what made the day?
What has the power to make the flower?
And what made the rain and made the snow?
Made us and made us want to know?

Love made the rainbow, the bird,
    and the summer sun.
Love made the mountain, the stars,
    each and every one.
Love made the sea and love made the land.
Love made the mighty
    and love made the very small.
Love made the world, made the people
Love made it all.

Lyrics by Josie Carey, Music by Fred Rogers

Who Shall I Be Today?

Who shall I be today, I say?
Who shall I be today, this day?
A dark horse, a light cow
A doggy or a cat.
A gray mouse, a blue owl
Or something like that.
There's so much to choose
And so much to be
That's why it's fun to be anybody.

Who shall I be today, I say?
Who shall I be today, this day?
A king or a queen
Or a doctor or a nurse.
A streetcar conductor, a witch with a curse.
There's so much to choose
And so much to be
That's why it's fun to be anybody.

One day I decided to be a fireman strong
I squirted water bravely and I rang
    the firehouse gong.
The next day was a Sunday so I
    most naturally
Just chose to be a singer
And I sang most gloriously.
Another day I baked a pie
Another wrote a book.
One day I was a fisherman
And fished without a hook.

Someday I'll be an engineer
Someday I'll dig a moat.
Someday I'll be a carpenter
Someday I'll drive a boat.
But . . .

Who shall I be today, I say?
Who shall I be today, this day?
A rich man, a poor man
A beggar man, a thief.
A doctor, a lawyer
A commander in chief.

There's so much to choose
And so much to be
That's why it's fun
To be anybody.
Anybody!

Good People Sometimes Do Bad Things

Good people sometimes think bad things,
Good people dream bad things
Don't you?
Good people even say bad things,
Once in a while we do.

Good people sometimes wish bad things,
Good people try bad things
Don't you?
Good people even do bad things,
Once in a while we do.

Has anybody said you're good lately?
Has anybody said you're nice?
And have you wondered how they could, lately,
Wondered once or twice?
    Did you forget that . . .

Good people sometimes feel bad things?
Good people want bad things
They do!
Good people even do bad things,
Once in a while we do.
Good people sometimes do!

You're Much More

You're not just your toes or your chin or your size
Not just a bit or a spot or a part
You're not just your outsides—
You're also your heart.

You see there's more than honking to geeses
And there's more to a cow than a moo.
When you add up all the pieces
There is more than we see to you.
When we put you all together
You're a beautiful, marvelous,
Spirited, lovely,
Wonderful one of a kind!

You're much more than your anger
And you're much more than your fist.
A closet's more than a hanger
And a fist has an arm and a wrist.
You're much more than your sadness
And you're much more than your frown.
More than a yell or a tap or a pout
More than a bellow or a slap or a doubt.
You're more than a moment, a feeling, a part,
You're more than an outside, you're inside your heart.

You're much much more than your anger
Much much more than your mind.
When they put you all together
You're a beautiful, marvelous, spirited, lovely,
Wonderful one of a kind!

I Need You

I need you so I can be your neighbor.
I need you so I can be your friend.
I need you so I can be who I am.
Who I am—I am your friend!

You need me so you can be my neighbor.
You need me so you can be my friend.
You need me so you can be who you are.
Who you are—you are my friend!

A bird needs air for its wings to fly.
A boat needs water to float.
A teacher needs students who want to know why.
An election needs a vote.
And a lining needs a coat.
Just as I need you so I can be who I am,
You need me so you can be yourself!

We both need each other
So we can be who we are.
Who we are—we are friends!

We both need each other
So we can be each other's—
We can be each other's friend.

I'm Interested in Things

I wish I could look inside the telephone.
I hear the voice, but I wish that I could see.
I'm interested in things like the telephone.
I'm interested in lots and lots of things.

I wish that I could look inside our trunk at home.
It's very old and I'm not supposed to look.
I'm interested in things like our trunk at home.
I'm interested in lots and lots of things.

I see the pictures in my book
And someday I'll know what the words all say.
If I wait long enough maybe I could cook.
Even hot things! Or drive the car or saw the wood
Or clean out the trunk or run the washing machine.
Someday I'll make my way okay.

Still, I wish that I could look inside big people's things.
Especially things that I'm not allowed to see.
I'm interested in all those big people things.
I'm interested in lots and lots of things.

But I can wait, and later on you'll see
I'll still be interested
always interested
In many things
In many, many things.

I Like to Be Told

I like to be told
When you're going away
When you're going to come back
And how long you will stay
How long you will stay
I like to be told.

I like to be told
If it's going to hurt
If it's going to be hard
If it's not going to hurt
I like to be told.

I like to be told
It helps me to get ready for all those things
All those things that are new.
I trust you more and more
Each time that I'm
Finding those things to be true.

I like to be told
'Cause I'm trying to grow
'Cause I'm trying to learn
And I'm trying to know.

I like to be told
I like to be told.

I Hope It Will Rain

I'm going to France in the morning.
I'm going by plane, by plane in the morning.
I hope it will rain 'cause I know how to say
Il pleut, it's raining, *il pleut*.

I'm going to Spain in the morning.
I'm going by plane, by plane in the morning.
I hope it will rain 'cause I know how to say
Está lloviendo, it's raining, *está lloviendo*.

I'm going to Germany in the morning.
I'm going by plane, by plane in the morning.
I hope it will rain 'cause I know how to say
Es regnet, it's raining, *es regnet*.

I'm going to Italy in the morning.
I'm going by plane, by plane in the morning.
I hope it will rain 'cause I know how to say
It's raining, *Piove*.

A Lonely Kind of Thing

It's a lonely thing
To think you might
Do something
That might make
    someone very mad.

It's a lonely thing
To think you might
Hurt someone
And that someone
Might be your mom or dad
Someone you like very much.

It's so lonely
Lonely
It's a very
        lonely,
        lonely

Kind of thing.

Sometimes People Are Good

Sometimes people are good
And they do just what they should.
But the very same people who are good sometimes
Are the very same people who are bad sometimes.
It's funny, but it's true.
It's the same, isn't it, for
Me and . . .

Sometimes people get wet
And their parents get upset.
But the very same people who get wet sometimes
Are the very same people who are dry sometimes.
It's funny, but it's true.
It's the same, isn't it, for
Me and . . .

Sometimes people make noise
And they break each other's toys.
But the very same people who are noisy sometimes
Are the very same people who are quiet sometimes.
It's funny, but it's true.
It's the same, isn't it, for
Me and . . .

Sometimes people get mad
And they feel like being bad.
But the very same people who are mad sometimes
Are the very same people who are glad sometimes.
It's funny, but it's true.
It's the same, isn't it, for
Me and . . .

Sometimes people are good
And they do just what they should.
But the very same people who are good sometimes
Are the very same people who are bad sometimes.
It's funny, but it's true.
It's the same, isn't it, for
Me . . . Isn't it the same for you?

I'm Tame

I don't growl anymore
I'm tame, I'm tame.
I don't prowl anymore
I'm tame.

I know right, I know wrong
I say thank you and please.
I remember to cover
My mouth when I sneeze.

I don't growl anymore
I'm tame, I'm tame.
I don't prowl anymore
I'm tame.

I use a napkin and fork
At each hamburger feast.
And act like a gentleman
Not like a beast.

I don't growl anymore
I'm tame, I'm tame.
I don't prowl anymore,
I'm tame.

Lyrics by Josie Carey, Music by Fred Rogers

Then Your Heart Is Full of Love

When your heart has butterflies inside it
Then your heart is full of love.
When your heart feels just like overflowing
Then your heart is full of love.

Love is fragile as your tears.
Love is stronger than your fears.
When your heart can sing another's gladness
Then your heart is full of love.

When your heart can cry another's sadness
Then your heart is full of love.
Love is fragile as your tears.
Love is stronger than your fears.

When your heart beats for a special someone
Then your heart is full of love.
When your heart has room for everybody
Then your heart is full of love.

Lyrics by Josie Carey, Music by Fred Rogers

The Truth Will Make Me Free

What if I were very, very sad
And all I did was smile?
I wonder after a while
What might become of my sadness?

What if I were very, very angry
And all I did was sit
And never think about it?
What might become of my anger?

Where would they go
And what would they do
If I couldn't let them out?
Maybe I'd fall, maybe get sick
Or doubt.

But what if I could know the truth
And say just how I feel?
I think I'd learn a lot that's real
About freedom.

I'm learning to sing a sad song when I'm sad.
I'm learning to say I'm angry when I'm very mad.
I'm learning to shout.
I'm getting it out!

I'm happy, learning
Exactly how I feel inside of me.
I'm learning to know the truth
I'm learning to tell the truth.
Discovering truth will make me free.

Wishes Don't Make Things Come True

One time I wished that a lion would come
And eat up my house and my street.
I was mad at the world and I wished that the beast
Would stomp everything with his big heavy feet
And eat everything with his big sharp teeth
And eat everything with his teeth.
But that wish certainly didn't come true
'Cause scary mad wishes don't make things come true.

One time I wished that a dragon would come
And burn up my Daddy's big store.
I was angry with him 'cause I wanted to play
And he went out the door to his store right away.
I wished that the dragon would burn his store,
I wished it would burn Daddy's store.
But that wish certainly didn't come true
'Cause scary mad wishes don't make things come true.

Everyone wishes for scary, mad things,
I'm sure that you sometimes do, too.
I've wished for so many and I can say
That all kinds of wishes are things just like play.
They're things that your thinking has made,
So wish them and don't be afraid.
I'm glad it's certainly that way, aren't you?
That scary mad wishes don't make things come true.
No kinds of wishes make things come true.

You've Got to Do It

You can make-believe it happens
Or pretend that something's true.
You can wish or hope or contemplate a thing you'd like to do.
But until you start to do it, you will never see it through.
'Cause the make-believe pretending just won't do it for you.
You've got to do it!

Every little bit, you've got to do it, do it, do it, do it.
And when you're through, you can know who did it
For you did it, you did it, you did it!
If you want to ride a bicycle and ride it straight and tall,
You can't simply sit and look at it 'cause it won't move at all.
But it's you who have to try it
And it's you who have to fall (sometimes)
If you want to ride a bicycle
And ride it straight and tall.
You've got to do it!

Every little bit, you've got to do it, do it, do it, do it.
And when you're through, you can know who did it
For you did it, you did it, you did it!
If you want to read a reading book
    and read the real words, too

You can't simply sit and ask the words
    to read themselves to you.
But you have to ask a person who can show you one or two
If you want to read a reading book
    and read the real words, too.
You've got to do it!

Every little bit, you've got to do it, do it, do it, do it.
And when you're through, you can know who did it
For you did it, you did it, you did it!
It's not easy to keep trying, but it's one good way to grow.
It's not easy to keep learning, but I know that this is so:
When you've tried and learned
You're bigger than you were a day ago.
It's not easy to keep trying, but it's one way to grow.
You've got to do it!

Every little bit, you've got to do it, do it, do it, do it.
And when you're through, you can know who did it,
For you did it, you did it, you did it!

You're the Only One

You're the only one who knows what you're thinking.
You're the only one.
You're the only one who knows how you're feeling.
You're the only one.

But if you'd like to share with another
That's for only you to do.
Since the only one who knows what you're thinking

Is you.

It's the People You Like the Most

It's the people you like the most
Who can make you feel maddest.

It's the people you care for the most
Who manage to make you feel baddest.

It's the people you like the most
Who can make you feel happiest!

It's the people you care for the most, most likely
Who manage to make you feel snappiest!

Love Is People

Love is people
Love is people needing people
Love is people caring for people
That is love.

Love's a little child
Sharing with another.
Love's a brave man
Daring to liberate his brother.

Love is people
Love is people needing people
Love is people caring for people
That is love.

And though some have costly treasure
It never seems to measure up
To people needing people
Caring for people
For that's love.

Love is people
People love.

You're Special

You're an ice cream cone
You're a lollipop
You're a baby chick
You're a pogo stick
You're a magic trick
You're a spinning top
You're special!

If someone asked me to relate
One reason you're so shiny
I'd really have to speculate
With eeny, meeny, miny.
You're a dancing doll
You're a shooting star
You're the foamy sea
You're a honeybee
You're a Christmas tree
You're a steel guitar
You're special!

You're a cowboy's horse
You're a baseball bat
You're a bright blue sky
You're a fishing fly
You're an apple pie
You're a pussy cat
You're special!

If someone asked me to confide
One reason you're so shiny
The only way I could decide
Is eeny, meeny, miny.
You're a swimming pool
You're a lightning bug
You're a smash homerun
You're a raisin bun
You're the noon day sun
You're a big bear hug
You're special!

Find a Star

Find a star, a star that seems just right
Wish with all your might, and then again
Find a star, don't let it out of sight
Wish with all your might again, and then . . .

Then find a wishbone
And find a four-leaf clover
And when the rain is over, find a rainbow
Go find a horseshoe
Go find a lucky penny
Just keep on wishing anyway.

Find a star, the same one every night
One that's shining bright and new for you
Find a star and cross your fingers tight
Then your wishes might come true.

Then find a wishbone
And find a four-leaf clover
And when the rain is over, find a rainbow
Go find a horseshoe
Go find a lucky penny
Just keep on wishing anyway.

Lyrics by Josie Carey, Music by Fred Rogers

A Smile's the Style

If you'd like to be in style
Here's a tip that's worth your while:
If you're happy, you'll look snappy
Just pick out your biggest smile.

No one really is impressed
With the way that we are dressed.
All the grinners are the winners
With a smile you'll look your best.

My suggestion is expression
Keep a bright look, it's the right look.
If your eyes glow and your teeth show
It's a sure sign that you feel fine.

You'll be welcome every place
And you'll win the fashion race.
If you're wearing and you're sharing
A real smile upon your face!

Lyrics by Josie Carey, Music by Fred Rogers

This Is Just the Day

If you've got an hour
Now's the time to share it.
If you've got a flower, wear it.
This is just the day.

If you've got a plan
Now's the time to try it.
If you've got an airplane, fly it.
This is just the day.

It's the day for seeing
All there is to see.
It's a day for being
Just you, just me.

If you've got a smile
Now's the time to show it.
If you've got a horn, then blow it.
It's the minute to begin it—
This is just the day.

Perfect Day

This day has really been unique
The wind and trees played hide-and-seek
The sun and clouds danced cheek-to-cheek
It's been a perfect day!

This day has really been so good
The sunshine shone just where it should
We all feel fine, let's knock on wood
It's been a perfect day!

Just ask the trees
Sheer perfection!
Ask the breeze
No objection!
Ask the bees
Near confection!
Sheer perfection, no objection, near confection, wow!

This day has really been the best
It certainly passed every test
From north to south and east to west
It's been a perfect day!

It's been a good day for a flower
It's been a good day for a tree
It's been a good day for a mushroom
    or a toadstool
It's been a good day for me.

This day has really been quite nice
The temperature took our advice
If you don't mind, we'll say it twice:
It's been a positively, absolutely perfect day!

I'm Proud of You

I'm proud of you
I'm proud of you
I hope that you're as proud as I am
Proud of you.
I'm proud of you
I hope that you are proud.

And that you're learning how important you are
How important each person you see can be
Discovering each one's specialty
Is the most important learning.

I'm proud of you
I'm proud of you
I hope that you're as proud as I am
Proud of you.
I'm proud of you
And I hope that you are proud of you, too!

Tomorrow

Tomorrow, tomorrow, we'll start the day
Tomorrow with a song or two.
Tomorrow, tomorrow, we'll start the day
Tomorrow with a smile for you.
I know tomorrow will be happy
And so tomorrow, make it snappy.
Tomorrow, tomorrow, it soon will be
Tomorrow and be our day, we'll say
A happy tomorrow to you!

It's Such a Good Feeling

It's such a good feeling
To know you're alive.
It's such a happy feeling
You're growing inside.
And when you wake up ready to say,
"I think I'll make a snappy new day!"
It's such a good feeling,
A very good feeling,
The feeling you know
You're alive!

It's such a good feeling
To know you're in tune.
It's such a happy feeling
To find you're in bloom.
And when you wake up ready to say,
"I think I'll make a snappy new day!"
It's such a good feeling
A very good feeling
The feeling you know
That we're friends.

Index of Song Titles

Index

Rogers produced *The Children's Corner*, a daily live hour-long visit with music and puppets. Rogers served as puppeteer, composer, and organist. In 1955, the show won the Sylvania Award for the best locally produced children's program in the country. It was on *The Children's Corner* that several regulars of *Mister Rogers' Neighborhood* made their debuts: Daniel Striped Tiger, X the Owl, King Friday XIII, Henrietta Pussycat, and Lady Elaine Fairchilde.

During his free time, Rogers attended the Pittsburgh Theological Seminary and the University of Pittsburgh's Graduate School of Child Development. He graduated from the seminary and was ordained a Presbyterian minister in 1963, charged with continuing his work with children and families through mass media. Later that year, Rogers was invited to create a program for the CBC in Canada that was called *Misterogers*. It was there that Fred Rogers made his on-camera debut as host.

When Rogers returned to Pittsburgh in 1966 with his family,

F red McFeely Rogers was born on March 20, 1928, in Latrobe, Pennsylvania. Rogers earned his bachelor's degree in music composition from Rollins College in Winter Park, Florida, in 1951. Upon graduation, he was hired by NBC as an assistant producer for *The Voice* of *Firestone* and, later, as floor director for *The Lucky Strike Hit Parade*, *The Kate Smith Hour*, and the *NBC Opera Theatre*. In 1952, Rogers married Joanne Byrd, a concert pianist and Rollins graduate.

In November 1953, at the request of WQED Pittsburgh, the nation's first community-sponsored educational television station, he incorporated segments of the CBC into a new series, which was distributed by the Eastern Educational Network. This series eventually became *Mister Rogers' Neighborhood*. In 1968 the program was made available for national distribution through the National Educational Television network (NET), which later became the Public Broadcasting Service (PBS).

Fred Rogers was the composer and lyricist of over two hundred songs, the author of numerous books for children, such as the First Experience series and the Let's Talk about It series, and the author of many books for adults, including *Mister Rogers Playtime Book*, *You Are Special*, *The Giving Box*, *Mister Rogers Talks with Parents*, and *Dear Mister Rogers: Does It Ever Rain in Your Neighborhood?*

Rogers received more than forty honorary degrees from distinguished educational institutions, among them Yale University, Carnegie Mellon University, Boston University, and his alma mater, Rollins College. He was awarded every major prize in television that he was eligible for, as well as many others from special-interest groups in education, communications, and early childhood development. In 1999 he was inducted into the Television Hall of Fame, and in 2002 President George W. Bush presented him with the Presidential Medal of Freedom, the nation's highest civilian honor. Rogers was recognized for his contribution to the well-being of children and for his career in public television that demonstrates the importance of kindness, compassion, and learning. "Fred Rogers has proven that television can soothe the soul and nurture the spirit and teach the very young," President Bush said.

Fred Rogers passed away on February 27, 2003, at his home in Pittsburgh, Pennsylvania. He is survived by his wife, Joanne Rogers, their two sons, and three grandsons.

Library of Congress Cataloging in Publication Number: 2018943034
Full CIP available on request.
ISBN: 978-1-68369-113-6
Printed in China
Typeset in Bookmania

Note: The songs on pages 17, 20, 28, 38, 44, 93, 112, 115, 128,
and 130 first appeared in *The Children's Corner*, hosted by Josie Carey
with puppets by Fred Rogers. These lyrics were written by Josie Carey,
to music by Fred Rogers.

Designed by Andie Reid and Doogie Horner
Illustrations by Luke Flowers
Editorial assistance by Rebecca Gyllenhaal
Production management by John J. McGurk

Quirk Books
215 Church Street
Philadelphia, PA 19106
quirkbooks.com
10 9 8 7 6 5

Opposite page: Fittingly, this book ends with an illustration of
Mr. Rogers on page 143. Fred Rogers considered the number 143
to be very special. He once said, "It takes one letter to say 'I' and
four letters to say 'love' and three letters to say 'you.' One hundred
and forty-three." He liked the number so much that he maintained
a weight of 143 pounds for the last thirty years of his life.

To learn more about Fred Rogers and the
Mister Rogers' Neighborhood TV show, visit MisterRogers.org.